Let Love Lead The Way

A Poetry Collection

Iris Mede

ISBN-13:9798779570121
ISBN-10: 1477123456

Cover design by: Art Painter
Library of Congress Control Number: 2018675309
Printed in the United States of America

This book is dedicated to all the writers, readers and artists. My your light shine on for all in the world to bask in and become inspired, for always.

"To love is to burn, to be on fire."
--JANE AUSTEN

Contents

I Want

I want to have the honor,
Of knowing you alone;
Better than anyone else,
Better than everyone I've known.

I want to know about you,
What lies inside your smile;
I want to find your secret place,
And linger there awhile.

I want your heart to open,
And your fears to confess,
All your private thoughts,
That have never been expressed.

I want to see inside your soul,
To view your passions and your dreams;
Anything and everything,
That makes you who you seem.

All this and much, much more,
I want to learn about you dear;
It may take a lifetime,
I will make it my career.

One Hundred Days

It's been one hundred days,
Since we first met,
And I've counted every day;
For I've been told,
That it takes that long,
Before you give your heart away.

I may be wrong about the days,
For I was never good at math,
And so many other things;
But the important thing to know,
Is that my heart I now bestow,
And everything that loving brings.

Love Is

Love is now defined
By everything that's you;
My life I intertwine,
To live my life with you!

The Flower

Is our love reality,
Or just a lovely dream?
Is it partly both,
Or something in between?
Who can really say
With utter certainty.

All flowers bloom to fall:
It is their destiny;
Our pairing is the blossoming
Of what our lives were to be.
How long will the flower bloom?
--That is up to you and me!

In The Dark

One day a woman took my hand
and led me to a place and a time
I had never imagined existed before.
After a time she brought me back
--but not all the way back.

That journey was about two hours long.
I took other journeys,
led by others, men and women,
that I met in the movies.

I needed those journeys
and I would ache to take them
if I had been away from them for long.
They were doors to new worlds.

They led me to understanding love.
I ache for their journeys now,
and seek still their places and faces
that leave me with something new.

A Feeling

Love --
It is a feeling like no other;
Like flowers basking in the sun;
Love emits its own bright color;
And exists to pleasure everyone.

Message

I wrote a message to you in the earth,
of my back yard. It simply read,
"I miss you."

I also wrote below in the same soft earth,
in the same back yard, this response back from you:
"So do I."

(I didn't want to take a chance
you would have a different reply.)

Beyond The Milky Way

In the early evening light,
The horizon for a stage,
My dreams take form in flight,
And reality slips away.

In the birthing of the night,
She appears from clouds and breeze
Her face forms full and bright,
Amid stars and galaxies.

She smiles and laughs so gaily,
In a way that is her own,
Then reaches out to touch me,
In a way I've never known.

I take her hand and rise,
To a place far away,
Then hold her close and fly,
Beyond the milky way.

As we reunite as one,
She and I are bound,
Beyond the milky way,
Where happiness is found.

A Couple

I saw a couple in a picture,
Smiling,
Knowingly at one another.

I want to have as much,
Sharing,
As that couple had together.

Fly

You are a fly, my darling,
Caught in the web I spin
Of sticky poems
That have drawn you
And captured you within
Layers and layers
Of papery thin words
That have subtle, musky scents
In their ink.

Each word
Wraps around you twice
To add to the cocoon
That is enveloping you,
Slowly, very slowly,
But completely
Into your chambered cell
By every tale that I tell
and there is nothing you can do!

Beauty

"She is beauty . . . is lovelier than daylight and more radiant than the sun. "

--Percy Blysshe Shelley

I stare at the poem, "She is beauty,"
and cannot believe
that Shelley didn't have you in mind
when he wrote those lines.
Shelley knew beauty of different kinds,
of their real outlines,
and the changes women make
in their many moods.

He seemed to know different kinds,
from the ordinary
and the necessary,
to the type that glows
from their mere outline.
who was fraud and who was real,
and the play of dark and bright
their moods reveal.

He knew the sacred game, as do I.
Along the way I learned it too,

but not its crowning elegance.
No, not until I met you.

I sit here in my chair, eyes closed,
waiting for the poem to say;
what it is it hears your movements
do twenty miles away.

I can see your face as your body aches
while speaking on the phone,
Your face now smiles attraction,
see your face as your body speaks
while talking a familiar smile
that says more than any poem.

You are beauty, with all the grace
of every beauty that has ever lived;
You don't know your power,
or the kind of allure that your body gives.
Power, or that like a flower,
it attracts and it fibs.

A Hat

I have made my love into a hat,
That you can wear all through the day;
Covered it with words of love,
That will array you when I am away.

It is made of plumes of passion,
That sweep in every way around;
Embroidered with hugs and kisses
That look and feel like down.

Wear it in the sunlight,
It will shelter and keep you;
Safe from fools that crave it,
But do not know it is only meant for you.

When I Met You

You were flower-like and I met you

in a meadow beneath a young pine branch.

Was it you or the meadow

that sent a lovely scent my way?

You were dressed in a linen skirt

that floated out from you,

and a bright silk blouse

that almost eclipsed the sun.

"Are you looking for your friend?"

you asked.

I said, "I was looking for you."

With your hand to your throat,

you said, "I have no friend, but I have a field.

This field, where all my life and existence is.

For the nearest town is forty miles away.

I live alone with my father,

who is a widower and forever sad.

I do not ever leave him,

for he is my dad.

But, I wish to follow you.

I will follow you even if it brings him pain.

I will follow you to the other side of my life

and will live under your roof

until you send me away.

Your hand is tender,

and your eyes are tender too.

Please let me go with you!"

"I carry nothing with me," I said,

"and nothing is my way."

With that I took a necklace

from my neck and gave it to you.

"That is the only thing of value,"

I said, "and you have it now."

Wear it for the times I'm not be near.

Always have it touching you:

It will be me touching you."

Maple Eyes

Your makeup's not as beautiful as you,
So you need not put on a disguise,
To glamorize what you have,
And will always have:
Such lovely eyes,
Maple eyes.

And your eyes do glow,
Amber-touched and sparkling,
Beautiful like a doe,
Maple eyes!

Lullaby for Lovers

Lovers become little children,
When love is in their heart.
So listen all lovers to this lullaby,
To learn how to keep your sweetheart.

Close your eyes now, I know you're sleepy,
And dream that love remains,
As good and perfect as it is now,
By following these lullaby refrains.

Lullaby and goodnight,
Tell them you love them, you do.
Lullaby and sleep tight,
They need to hear that from you.

Lullaby and goodnight,
Never stop listening and talking,
Lullaby and sleep tight,
Always do more giving than taking.

Lullaby and goodnight,
Always show affection with a kiss,
Lullaby and sleep tight,
And never let a day pass when you miss.

Lullaby and goodnight,
Argue quite less than you're prone,
Lullaby and sleep tight,

Just agree to disagree,
then leave it alone.

Lullaby and goodnight,
Give them the treasure of your time,
Lullaby and sleep tight,
Because that's what they want
most the time.

I know you're almost asleep,
And your sweetheart in your dreams
you'll see,
But hear this one last promise to keep.
And commit it to your memory:
For love that's so right,
And that will never end,
Always treat your sweetheart,
Like your very, very best friend!

You

You came into my life when I needed you.
It was as if you knew
exactly what I was going through.

We talked and you said everything
that I wished you would say,
everything I could only pray you'd say.

Cat People

There is a cat in her.
I can hear her purr.

Sometimes she's a sleek black panther,
graceful and lovely,
gliding through the night.
She's soft and seductive then,
but do not raise her fur.

Sometimes she's a playful Persian cat,
frisky and feminine,
frolicking through the day.
She's cute and clever then,
and nothing's too good for her.

Sometimes she's a mangy alley cat,
cunning and quick,
slinking through back yards.
She has no conscience then,
and will cuff her claws in a blinding whir.

Sometimes she's a haughty lioness,
proud and defiant,
who rules the entire jungle.
She's strong, but agile then,
so do not make her stir.

There is a cat in her.
I can hear her purr.

Sometimes her cat creeps in subtly
and seduces me.
Her scent wafts across my senses
and I quiver with ecstasy.

Sometimes she springs from hiding
and attacks me.
Her assault is so savage.
Oh, how wild she can be!

Sometimes she's just a kitten
and I can control her,
Even though I realize
I am not the master; it is really her.

But sometimes she's filled with strength
and overpowers me;
And I race to the safety
of my mouse hole, to which she has a key.

There is a cat in her.
I can hear her purr.

Sometimes she toys with me,
batting my soul back and forth
between her front paws,
Catching it by the tail
at that precise instant
in which it would have been free.

Sometimes she soothes me,
and sings to me softly,
and caresses me,
Until I find relief
from the fever
that she has given me.

Sometimes she's glorious
and takes me with her
away from the ordinary
away from all that burdens me
to heights of ecstasy
that mere mortals never see.

Sometimes, oh, sometimes...
There is a cat in her.
I can hear her purr.

In Your Mind

In your mind please put aside
in some corner,
a thought from me
to save as a memory
to think about if you
have nothing else to do.

Remind yourself of our times
doing simple things,
and that the most simple things
we've done,
are far better than
the best things we have ever done.

Dreaming

Are you dreaming? I hope that you are. You lie here on the bed next to me with your hands up next to your face and your legs curled up under you. You have a warm half-smile on your face and the word "tenderness" seems to fit you perfectly.

You've been asleep now for about twenty minutes. I noted a soft whisper of breath from you that signaled sleep about that long ago. You have a soft purr to your breath now. But, are you dreaming?

Dreaming of. . . .
  children,
  animals,
  and me.

I touch your shoulder gently with my hand and then move it down to your waist. It is a waist that breaks hearts -- both of women and men. You move languidly. Was it in response to my touch? Maybe. But, but, are you dreaming?

Dreaming of. . . .
  children,
  animals,
  and me.

Your beauty does not disappear at night. It becomes softer and more natural. You are the most beautiful woman I have ever met. Could any movie star be more beautiful than you? I think not. For all I know, the fabled Helen of Troy could not have been more beautiful.

As I look upon you in the semi-dark of night your hair is dark as well. I imagine you with your blond hair, and then turn it to red in my mind. I wonder what your hair would be like in braids. Or perhaps longer, or shorter. I imagine all the possibilities. Oh, you are so beautiful that no change in your hair color or style would matter. But, are you dreaming?

Dreaming of. . . .
    children,
    animals,
    and me.

There are so many dreams that you might dream. Some of troubles and some of joy. Your life has not been an easy one. Yet you sleep the sleep of rest and comfort. Am I in small part the cause of that? I like to thing so. But, are you dreaming?

Dreaming of. . . .
    children,
    animals,
    and me.

You say that you never dream. Everybody dreams. You just never remember yours. Are they that secret, or that morose?

Oh, Darling, I want to cry out to you: Please be comforted and dream. Please dream. Please dream. Please dream.

Please dream of . . . .
    children,
    animals,
    and me.

Can't Come Back

When we made love the first time,
We didn't stop,
At the point we knew.
We went on to climb far higher,
Beyond the top,
And shot right through.

How would we know the first time,
Limits would end,
And our perceptions would crack;
We only set out to find some fun,
But went too far,
And can't come back.

Rabbit

"I will always love you and take care of you, said the girl to her lover who had been turned into a gray rabbit by a sorcerer. She then put a precious collar around his neck and fed him flower petals." --
Grimm's Fairy Tales

I come to you in the night,
silent and soft of step,
and feast each night from your garden,
as if I have been invited.

I pick the most tender leaves
and succulent of blossoms.
Though you have labored
planting and tending my food,
you did not expect to feed
a small gray rabbit.

I come like a refugee each night,
defying fences and cars
and risking death on the way.
Should you know of me?

Might you fit me with a precious collar
and feed me flower petals?

I would put down my ears
and snuggle in your lap.

Love Is

Love is now defined
By everything that's you;
My life I intertwine,
To live my life with you!

In The Park

In the park, on a grassy mound,
under a shade tree,
I stand beside a woman.
Her hair's made of spun white gold,
spun from the sunlight that it rides upon.

Other women see her. Other men see her.
She is different from them.
She is dressed differently,
she talks differently,
and she hears differently.

Her skin is even different from theirs.
It is delicate and must be well protected.
In the sunlight it is almost translucent.
Some might call it "milky."
Others might call it "porcelain."
It's all in the way you see it.

We stand in the hot sun talking.
It is very hot.
She appears to be swaying in the hot sun.
She faces away from the sun,
but keeps talking.
Sunlight suits her,
but she doesn't think so.

Her hair is medium long.
It is too hot for this sun.
She has a hat, but it makes her hotter still.
She has a dilemma: keep the hat on and be hot,
or take the hat off and get sunburned.
She keeps the hat on.

She meets many people.
Moving easily among them,
seeming to men beautiful,
and to women...?
Do they think that she's my type?
Is she my type? Who is my type?

We talk easily afterward.
There is a warm familiarity between us.
I feel that she is "my type." Miraculous,
I call it, and I can call her "my type,"
even if no one else could:
She is a woman-who-is-my-type.

A Lonely Day

It's a lonely day
Sitting here without you;
So long a day and I'm so very sad
To be so lonely and miserable without you.

I Memorize

I memorize you,
each time we part,
so that I can keep,
that last moment with you,
locked away,
in my memory.

The way you look,
while walking away,
and the way you wink,
back over your shoulder,
and smile once more,
over at me.

Hours later,
and days later,
--and forever,
I will remember you,
looking at me that way
that very special way.

A Feeling

Love is a feeling like no other:
Like flowers radiating in the sun,
It emits glorious bright colors,
And lives for its glow to be done

You

You came into my life when I needed you.
It was as if you knew
exactly what I was going through.

We talked and you said everything
that I wished you would say,
everything I could only pray you'd say.

Different?

We were born in different lands,
under different skies and moons.
We were raised under far different clouds
and far different rains in June.

But did we see the same shining stars
and the same bright sun at noon?

We had neither the same language
nor the same landscape too.
But did our hearts beat the same
even back then too?

Did the climates from which we came
leave us with the same gentle
and melancholy moods?

And where did the passions
that we both possess spring forth
in such generous ways.

We both know how to love and suffer.
Are those the same lessons
that we both had to learn?

The ardor of our love still gives you pause

and still disturbs you yet today.
The fervor of your desire frightens you
in so many ways that your mind does faze.

You do not know whether to accept
the passion or throw it all away.
When one has no similar past,
one wonders if it ever will last.
But what about the desire,
with fire and the feelings that amaze.

You do not know if you truly love me,
even before the question of my love for you,
and you may never really know
the truth of either one of these.

But consider the passion that we feel,
it is quite real and it is a rock
that firmly stands quite tall.
It will never fall!

Your Equine Eyes

Your equine eyes are everywhere,
Much larger than they have to be,
Haunting me and taunting me,
Those deep dark liquid equine eyes of thee.

Each Time

Each time
that I see you
I always find you
much more desirable
and much more wonderful
each time.

Each time
that I leave you
I find it much harder
and much more difficult
to turn around and leave you
each time.

Love Walked In

Do you recall a song,
by George and Ira Gershwin
called, "Love Walked In"?
Well, my dear,
they didn't quite
get it right
in the lyrics of that song.

Love didn't, "Walk right in
and drive the shadows away."
It was more like you
let me see
something beyond shadows.

Love didn't, "Walk right in
and bring my sunniest day."
It was like I had never
even seen the sun.

The Gershwin's wrote,
"One magic moment
and my heart seemed to know
that love said 'Hello,'
though not a word was spoken,"
and they were almost right.

The magic moment happened,

but it happened later.
Later also did I take,
"One look and forgot the gloom of the past;
One look and found my future at last.
One look and found a world so new
When love walked in with you."

I did, of course, but just not the way
the Gershwin's wrote.
They were geniuses of song,
But they were not geniuses of life.

A Rhyme

This is just a simple rhyme,
To think about from time to time;
When you need anything at all,
Don't hesitate to give a call;
Count on me to always come through,
Count on me to be there for you.

I Should

I should tell you,
when loving thoughts fill my head,
in the bed or in the bath,
but I don't.

I could tell you,
so much about my love for you,
and the things that we could do,
but I won't.

Some things are only necessary,
if at all, when love is not as strong,
or it feels like it needs fixing,
but it's not.

Sleeping Beauty

The deep night reigns
With its nocturnal hue
As it envelops and wraps
Mind, soul and body too.

You eyes have just closed,
A short time and a long kiss ago.
After our loving,
After we made each other glow.

You lie there so lovely,
For just me to see
As nighttime has turned
you into my sleeping beauty.

Your Eyes

If I had never seen your eyes,
How different my life would be,
Without the love I prize.
That you offer me.

If I hadn't memorized
Your wonderful, loving face,
What would I have to fill my heart,
--just empty space.

But my memory is full
And there is no wasted space,
It is filled with all I've fantasized,
Before I had ever seen your eyes.

When I Drive

When I drive away from you,
I feel a heavy weight fall on me;
Like coal dust floating over me, choking me,
I cannot seem to breathe the air.
I call out for you to the caring stars,
And shout to the witness of the wind,
That you are the reason I've come this far.

Mile after mile, car after car,
Each one seems to toll and tally
The growing distance from my heart;
The lights of the cars prick my eyes,
So that I can no longer see your face;
And I want to wound myself and die,
Upon the sharp edges of the night.

Tell Me

Tell me:
Was Helen more beautiful
Than thee
When she launched 1000 ships?

Tell me:
If the waves still drift shoreward
On your oyster shell
That inspired Botticelliís Eve?

The Night

The night begins, slowly.
It has crept quietly in
as the day has vanished.

I have whispered your name,
as if the sound of your name
can make you appear.

Low clouds are closing in,
engulfing the hillsides here,
erasing the view of everything,

but the silhouette of you.

You shimmer there,
your essence among the clouds and dew.

But, where are you?
I need your touch, so very, very much.

I hear the coyotes call.
They're searching too.

Please take my hand.
It's reaching out for you.

Please understand,
my life belongs with you.

My Picture

Resting my head on one hand
I prop up in bed and look at you
as you stand at the window
your head cocked in appraisal of the view.

The wind stirs lightly
and water gurgles,
--ordinary things that go on
that seem to now include you.

You are part of my routine now,
my ordinary life,
as much as is the man next door.

He walked over to me and angrily said,
"That tree has to go." "It will grow too big
and spoil my view," even if that takes 20 years.

This same man who said to me --I don't know
where he came from, Minnesota or wherever,
--that my dead leaves blow into his yard.

Should I send my leaves to obedience school
to have them learn to behave properly for him?

He could have come here from anywhere,
but he is in my life now, as you are, a fixture
and an integral part of my existence.

Standing there at the window,
you seem to be an extension of me
--and I also don't know
where you came from,
from upstate you told me,
but I believe you have fallen from the sky,
into my life and into my heart one night.

Share

You, sweet darling dear,
Who has shared with me more joys
Than I have ever known,
Please come and share with me
More joys yet still unknown.

Share with me a dwelling-place
Where we may find our peace;
Hand in hand and face to face,
We'll make our love a masterpiece.

Happiness

It's called Happiness -- and I've been there!
Taken in hand by you, to that magic place,
I've reveled in that feeling
while looking at your face.

It's called Happiness -- and I've been there!
You with the sparkling eyes
and with flaxen flowing hair,
You took me with disbelief and doubt
and I found bliss everywhere.

It's called Happiness -- and I've been there!
I know I don't deserve such joy,
for few ever really do,
But it was my luck to find such a place
and a special one like you.

It's called Happiness -- and I've been there!
It's called Happiness -- and I've been there!
It's called Happiness -- and I've been there
with you!

No Robin

No robin wears a more brilliant brown,
So proudly on its chest,
Than the Autumn brown of your eyes,
That glisten like a crest.

They turn chestnut, then golden bronze
As the light changes hue,
And glitter like the finest jewels.
When I'm facing you.

Random Moments

I saw you, darling, in the shop today,
and I had to say, "I love you," in your ear.
I also said it in the cafe where we stopped
Later. I hope you don't mind these

Random moments, whether at the movies,
or while walking along a bridle path, they
are all times when love swells in me and I
have to just let it vent from me. Yes these

Random moments occur spontaneously at
anytime and anywhere. Yesterday a man
grinned at me in the shop, apparently he
had also heard. And I was proud. At

Random moments I love you so very, very
much that I want to say it loud and let the
world know how I feel: It feels strong and
so real. Sometimes life comes to a halt for

Random moments, as time almost stops on
some quite ordinary days, made special by
the way my spirit gets renewed and by the
way my love gains breathing space; I need

Random moments all my days.

Golden Hue

A golden hue
circles your head
arising from your bed
till you lie again
after your day's end
over all that you do.
But knowing you
it merely mocks
and is just a pair of socks
that you must wear
without really a care
of the special you.

Orchid

There once was an orchid
that bloomed
on a South Sea island,
tall, beautiful and fragrant,
with all the colors of a sunset
from reddish pink to jasmine white
on its sweeping, soaring perfect petals

It was so utterly beautiful
that once an elder
looked upon it and jumped
into a volcano to his swift death
because he would not want his eyes
to ever gaze again at anything less perfect.

That orchid was you,
darling,
in one of your other lives.

On Our Wedding Night

The Cosmos held a party,
On our wedding night;
All creation was invited,
To every star's delight.

The room was filled with creatures
That weren't often asked to teas,
Boar hogs and robins
sat down with centipedes.

In candlelight and splendor,
The guests toasted you and me;
They wished us long and happy lives,
Saying we were meant to be!

About The Author

Iris Mede

She is an indi writer and editor for a Los Angeles-based online magazine. This is her first venture into poetry.